WALK THE WINNING WAYS OF GOLF'S GREATESTS

How the Greatest Players in Golf Found Inspiration to Win and Their Advice to Young Golfers.

A Treasury of Motivational Stories and Quotes from Arnie, Nicklaus, Tiger, Phil, Rory, D.J., Justin Thomas, Rickie Fowler, Jason Day, Bubba, and many more

Presented by The Team at Golfwell

GOLFWELL

Published by: Pacific Trust Holdings NZ Ltd., 2017

Black and White Edition

Praises received:

"Perfect advice direct from Golf's Greats for hard-working young golfers aspiring to play golf at the highest level. Inspiring, thought provoking, and an entertaining book. Liked the comments of what the world's best golfers said about each other!"

-C. Charleston, Chicago

"Walk the Winning Ways of Golf's Greatests" gave me a clear picture on how the greats did it and gained confidence. A different side of the nature of the game revealed in one book – the practical side! Thank you."

-R Andersen, Atlanta

"This book is an inspiring read and wish it was put out earlier. Great insight and advice from the Pros on how to win on Tour…. Liked learning how the past Champions were inspired and how they did it. Loved the confidence building techniques and how to maintain the confidence to win."

-J. Russo, Toledo

INTRODUCTION

Jack Nicklaus said, "Confidence is the most important single factor in this game, and no matter how great your natural talent, there is only one way to obtain and sustain it: hard work."

This book is for young golfers to help develop confidence and the right attitudes to enjoy golf more, as well as to compete better, and even make professional golf a career.

It's for young golfers who want to make the high school golf team or get that college scholarship.

It's also for any golfer who has the ability to compete with the best on tour, but just keeps failing to qualify, or keeps missing cuts.

Generally, it's for anyone who wants to improve their golf and confidence level, or help them calmly deal with bad or embarrassing shots, and make golf more enjoyable no matter what your age may be.

Dr. Bob Rotella said, "Play a shot confidently, and the body performs at its graceful best."

"Play a shot while doubting your ability to pull it off and the body often loses its rhythm, grace and timing."

Most agree having the right attitude, and a good confidence level makes your subconscious automatically allow your body to perform well in the split second it takes to impact a golf ball.

Young golfers (as well as all golfers) will get insights from the greatest players playing at the highest level.

A treasury of motivational stories and quotes from golf's greatest, this book tells you how the best in golf got to where they are and the hard work they put in to get there.

And, you get ways on how to develop and maintain a good confidence level in whatever career you choose in your life.

Enjoy! And remember, you can be the best golfer!

"Never bend your head. Always hold it high.

Look the world straight in the face."

-Helen Keller

Contents

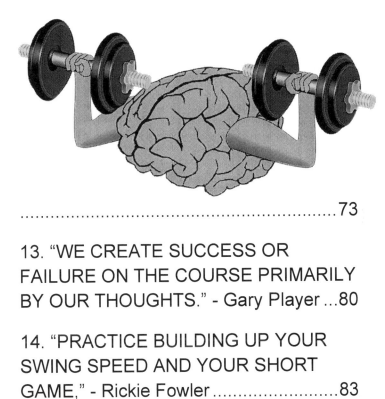

20. "I COULD MAKE A PRETTY FAIR APPRAISAL OF THE WORTH OF AN OPPONENT BY TAKING A GOOD

30. "WHEN I'M PLAYING MY BEST AND FIND MYSELF IN CONTENTION ON SUNDAYS, IT'S USUALLY WHEN I'M NOT THINKING ABOUT MY SWING, BUT RATHER TRUSTING MY SETUP

1. "WHENEVER THE HEAT'S ON, MY WHOLE LIFE, I'VE JUST KIND OF LEARNED TO FOCUS A LITTLE MORE," - Jordan Spieth

"When I first met him, I tell you I'll never forget it."

"I looked right at him, and he looked at me, and I thought I was looking at Wyatt Earp."

"He looks at you like he's going to gun you down."

- Ben Crenshaw on Jordan Spieth

Jordan Spieth was born into an athletic family.

"My dad played college baseball, my mom played college basketball, and my brother played basketball for Brown University."

Jordan said, "I played baseball for a while as a pitcher (a southpaw), but gave it up as a teenager to focus on golf."

"I was a pitcher, and my dad played in college." Jordan said it was difficult to tell his dad he wanted to play golf.

"The hardest day of my life was telling him I was going to quit to focus more on golf."

"But with golf, I felt like the game can't be perfected, and that motivated me."

Another inspiration for Jordan has been his sister, Ellie, who has a genetic disorder and has special needs. He wanted to help her and is helping her and others through the "Jordan Spieth Family Foundation" which helps those with special needs as well as Junior Golf and military families.

Tiger Woods also inspired Jordan. "There's nobody that had more influence on my golf game than Tiger."

"He may still have a lot of good years ahead of him in my mind."

"Obviously, it's frustrating for him, but we haven't seen the end of him."

"When I was 11 years old, I watched Tiger hole out that amazing birdie chip in on the 16th hole at Augusta in 2005," said Jordan.

"That chip made me want to literally walk outside and for hours on end practice chipping."

Jordan adds, "It made me want to go and hit those chip-spinners because I always loved hitting those, and I was just starting to develop those at that age."

Jordan stays positive to keep himself up. "If you are going to talk negative about a place, you're almost throwing yourself out to begin with because golf is a mental game."

Confidence and results comes from hard work according to Jordan.

Jordan set goals for himself. "I had two goals."

"I wanted to win the Masters, and I wanted to be the best player in the world. Those were my two lifelong goals."

"Having accomplished some of my major goals in the sport of golf, why shouldn't I work as hard as I can to attain other goals I think about."

So, Jordan, as good as he is at golf, keeps a healthy attitude to keep on winning and he drives himself to become better and better.

Jordan's advice to young golfers is, "If you can hit a good drive, the game of golf is a lot easier."

He recommends being sure you choose the right driver.

"On the tee, you should feel comfortable when you take your stance and look down at your driver."

"I've played with the right driver for some time and it makes me feel comfortable using it."

"When I feel comfortable, I have confidence in my tee shot and that makes the game easier."

Jordan believes from the age of 10 to 16, it's important to be among friends who love to play golf and socialize and learn the game together, and compete against each other.

That's what he did and he wasn't the best player among them. He had a strong desire to be better which he still has today.

Jordan played Junior Ryder Cup and with all of the things he has accomplished, he's said, "PGA of America has been very good to me; I played the Junior Ryder Cups, and those go down as some of the best experiences I've ever had on a golf course."

Jordan's advice to young golfers for bunker play is, "In greenside bunkers, the big thing is to adapt your stance to the shot."

"It's rare that you get a flat lie in the sand, so I make sure to align my body to the slope."

So, once you have your alignment, Jordan says, "I blast the ball out by splashing the sand under it."

He adds, "Stats are important to me, especially the ones related to scoring."

"You're going to miss fairways and greens, so how you play from the sand really matters."

Jordan said the transition to play the PGA Tour is getting easier for younger players.

"The generation that I'm in is extremely talented, and those that are still in school, my peers that are my age, will be out here really soon."

"You guys will see. You will make a pretty easy transition on the PGA Tour."

Jordan says American Junior Golf is a help to young players. "Without the AJGA, it would be very difficult for the college coaches to find us."

"Every junior golfer around the country knows about the AJGA and knows that's the way to get to college. And, the way to get beyond college."

Jordan has a winning attitude and tries his best in every tournament. "If you're in it enough, you're going to be on the good end and bad end of those situations, so keep putting yourself in contention."

"When you're on the good end, you'll be able to enjoy it even more having experienced the other side of it."

2. "THE BEST THING ABOUT ME IS THAT I NEVER GIVE UP," says Jason Day

"When I taught Jason how to play golf and showed him how to do something, say one of the fundamentals of golf, Jason would do it over and over again and over again."

"That quality was something none of the other students had."

"The other students would get bored with a fundamental and move on, but Jason kept at it until he had it completely mastered."

> *-Colin Swatton, Jason Day's Coach*

When Jason Day was interviewed by David Feherty about his early years learning golf, he explained it wasn't easy. His father died when Jason was 12.

"I remember not having a hot water tank, so we had to use a kettle for hot showers."

Jason adds, "So, you know, we would put the kettle on and go have a shower, and then my mum would come bring three or four kettles in, just to heat them up."

"And it would take five, 10 minutes for every kettle to heat up."

Jason said he got the "Never give up" attitude from his father.

"My dad was the way he was, but he also gave me a motto: never say die."

His dad told him when he was very young to, "Keep pushing and pushing, fighting until the end."

"He put it in my head that you're always going to fight, and you're always going to beat them."

Jason got into schools which featured a golf program and Jason met and learned from coach, Colin Swatton, who later caddied for Jason on tour.

Jason was influenced by Tiger Woods' book, "How I Play Golf" (he borrowed it), and was determined to match Tiger's scores. "I practiced in the early morning, at lunch and in the evening continually," said Jason.

Tiger and Jason have a good relationship to this day.

Jason said, "To be able to have him as someone to bounce things off when you don't quite have the answers?"

"Tiger has the experience and the knowledge of finishing and playing and winning a lot of tournaments."

And, he adds, "Tiger's advice and experience is the best sort of advice that you can get out there."

Tiger tells Jason whenever he's in the lead on any round in a tournament, he needs to have, "Patience and aggression, and try to extend the lead by one or two shots every day."

Tiger also said to him, "If it's not going your way, suck it up and just get it done somehow."

"Patience and aggression." Jason explains, "Sometimes that's what you need to have to win golf tournaments, especially when you do have the lead and that's what Tiger's done, and he's won so many times with patience and aggression.

"I practice a lot and golfers need to have mental toughness since it builds confidence, especially in junior golfers."

"You've got to be tough to earn the wins, they're not given to you," Jason says.

"It's a lot about just trying to get better mentally."

Jason points out how important it is to believe in yourself, "If you don't believe in yourself, somewhere or another, you sabotage yourself."

Jason realizes confidence levels go up and down.

"It really is amazing that some days you'll come out and you'll feel like you can beat anyone."

"And then some days you come out and you've got no confidence in the world, and you can't break an egg with a hammer."

Jason doesn't like losing, "It just flat-out sucks losing. It really - it doesn't feel good."

But, he also points out the positive side of losing, "I'm getting better and better each year that I'm playing golf on the world stage."

"And finishing runner-up only teaches you how to continue being patient - something that is key to the game of golf."

"Golf is an individual sport," Jason said.

"I think I definitely like the solitude of golf. I have always practiced by myself."

"It's just because that's where I can do most of my work."

In other words, Justin said, "The most efficient work is done when I am by myself, and I think I just find a little bit of peace on the golf course."

Jason finds peace by himself, "It's just you and yourself and your thoughts."

Jason advised young golfers to get enough sleep.

"Rest is huge because if you're sleep-deprived, that can definitely run into the mental side of the game."

"You can definitely hurt your game if you're tired playing tournament golf."

Jason is dedicated to winning, "I want to win every single tournament that I'm playing in."

But he knows winning doesn't happen every time. He's told young golfers, "It's O.K. to fail."

"It's about learning, because obviously, I learn more when I fail than when I win."

Jason adds, "Just keep putting yourself there."

Jason knows if you keep putting yourself there, confidence will come.

"Once I started saying to myself, 'Just keep putting yourself there' and really believing in that, over time, it just gradually gave me confidence."

And, Jason said, "When you have a lot of confidence and you feel like nobody can beat you, it's game over for everyone else."

Jason keeps a realistic attitude.

"I'm just here for this one purpose; and that's to try and get better each and every day and try and win as much as I can, while I can."

And, when Jason is going into the final round leading the tournament, he loves it.

"I'd much rather have that pressure on me than to be at the end of the field and no one expecting you to win."

"That's the kind of pressure that you've got to enjoy and love."

And when Jason retires from golf, he said his thoughts will be along these lines:

"At the end of my career, am I going to say I did well, but I didn't give it my all?"

"I'd be very, very angry with myself if I didn't give 100 percent."

Jason said, "If I gave my all and I got to whatever point in the world I got to, I could look back and at least say, I did the best I could."

"Self-confidence, A feeling of trust in one's abilities, qualities, and judgment."

– English Oxford Dictionary

3. "DEDICATE YOURSELF TO BEING GOOD IN ALL ASPECTS OF THE GAME," says Ray Floyd

"As a kid in Fayetteville, N.C., I played golf all day, every day, a lot of it by myself," said Ray Floyd.

"I spent hundreds of hours around the greens at Cape Fear Valley, the course my dad owned, hitting every shot I could think of - the one-hop-and-release, the chip that lands dead, the explosion from a bad lie."

Ray won his first PGA Tournament in Florida when he was 20 years old. That year, he was named PGA Rookie of the year.

He went on to win 4 Majors and 22 PGA Tournaments.

We wrote to Ray Floyd and asked what influenced him the most in becoming the great golfer he is, and he replied,

"My father was a golf professional and my teacher, and he inspired me to give my full concentration and effort in everything I tried to accomplish in sports."

"I was a pretty good baseball player as a young man, and seriously contemplated a professional career in that sport, but my Dad encouraged me to focus on being excellent in one sport rather than being pretty good at two."

We asked Ray for his advice to young golfers and he said, "My advice to any young golfer who wants to excel at the sport is to dedicate yourself to being good in all aspects of the game."

Ray wrote, "Everyone, particularly young players, likes to hit the ball hard and long."

Ray pointed out the important part is, "But the real scoring part of our sport takes place from 60 yards in, so I would encourage youngsters to spend as much time learning how to chip and putt as they do with their driving."

"The finesse shots around the green and short approaches were one of the real strengths of my game, and in my prime, I felt I could outplay anyone in the game around the green," Ray remarked.

Doug Ford was an influence on Ray on his chipping ability. "Doug Ford was one of the first of the old pros I saw during my first full year on tour, in 1963."

Ray said, "To this day, he's the best chipper I've ever seen."

"One thing Doug did was get the ball onto the green and rolling right away, keeping it as low as possible."

Ray added, "Doug didn't hit his chips higher than was absolutely necessary."

But now most say, Ray was the best at chipping.

Steve Williams, who caddied for Ray Floyd, as well as Greg Norman, Tiger Woods, and currently caddying for Adam Scott, has been in the arena with the world's greatest golfers for 40 years. He's seen, up and close, the best players in golf, a lot of styles and more golf talent than most people ever experience.

Steve, a member of the Caddie Hall of Fame, wrote this about Ray in his book, "Out of the Rough",

"Raymond was the most masterful chipper of the ball I've ever seen."

"He could chip the ball from anywhere, using any club, and he had great vision for how the ball would land and roll once it was on the green."

Ray says, practice is vitally important. "Dedication to practicing those shots gave me confidence, and that confidence in my ability helped me win a lot of golf tournaments."

And, Ray never gave up. "I've never not tried on a shot. I may shoot 80, but I'm giving every swing 100 percent." *Sleepy ridge experence*

His late wife, Maria, was a great inspiration and she wouldn't let him ever give up.

When Ray was 31 years old, he started thinking about doing something other than golf, but Maria said he could, of course, change careers but emphasized, "No matter what you do, always give it 100%."

Ray went on to win 16 more tour events.

"Success gives you an advantage." Ray has said, "When you're the best, and you know you're the best, and your contemporaries know you're the best, that's a terrific edge."

"Self-confidence is the most attractive quality a person can have."

"How can anyone see how great you are if you can't see it yourself?"

- Anonymous

4. "YOU DON'T HEAR THE BEST PLAYERS IN THE WORLD BASHING THEMSELVES OUT THERE," says Justin Thomas

"He was very smart, very grounded."

"He always wanted to know how to practice, what I think about golf shots, golf courses, how to get around a little bit on the Tour."

"He picked it up fast."

> *- Kenny Perry, 14 time PGA Tour Winner who knew Justin as a teen.*

Justin's father is Mike Thomas, a golf pro in Kentucky.

"My dad encouraged me to get better and better and I enjoyed playing the game."

Kenny Perry was a friend of Justin's dad and competed against Mike in college, and they remained friends and Kenny watched Justin grow up. Kenny and Justin still converse today.

Justin has found memories of growing up at Harmony Landing.

"The 16th hole at Harmony Landing is 144 yards."

"For years, it was the only hole I could reach in regulation growing up," Justin said.

One amazing fact that Justin points out, "When I was 6, I made a hole-in-one there, hitting my cut-down driver. My dad and grandpa made an ace there as well."

So, Justin adds, "Three generations scoring aces on the same hole. How many families can say that?"

Justin says, "The top players aren't going around working on how to walk confidently. It's more of a demeanor and a mindset when you're out there." "it's realizing that when things go bad, you are good enough to overcome that."

Justin adds, "There's no reason you can't go around feeling like that all the time too."

Justin talks about his grandfather. "My grandpa is full of stories and simple wisdom. I never tire of hearing him talk golf."

Justin learned his grandfather's philosophy of the game. His grandfather had a saying, "Some days it's chickens, and some days it's feathers."

Justin said, "That means, no matter how good you are, you can't be at your best all the time."

"The nature of the game is that you'll run hot and cold, and I keep that in mind."

Justin tries to play within his game even though he sees others hit longer drives.

"Luke List hits it so stupid far, he might be on a level even above those guys like Dustin Johnson, Bubba Watson, Tony Finau, etc.,"

Justin said, "I watch Luke List and think, If I could do that, it would be wedge city on every hole."

But Justin added, "I get those thoughts out of my mind very quickly. No sense drooling over something you can't have."

Justin's best advice for young people is having confidence.

"When I'm out there I like to feel confident," Justin said.

"Because if you can't feel confident about yourself, how are you going to perform well?"

5. "UM, YEAH, 15 YEAR OLDS DON'T LEAD AT AN LPGA EVENT ALL THE TIME. BUT LIKE I'VE SAID, I'VE BEEN PLAYING REALLY GOOD GOLF AND I'M CONFIDENT WITH MY GAME," said Lydia Ko

"I think she will always be an inspiration to young golfers, to women that play the game, even men that play the game and I don't think that will ever change."

- Brooke Henderson

As she grew up, Lydia Ko practiced every day at golf courses north of Auckland. Most everyone knew her very well.

Lydia was friendly, laid back and talked with anyone.

Guy Wilson began coaching her when she was 5 years old.

Lydia was quietly confident about her abilities. And, she felt there wasn't anything special about her talent. Quiet and confident, she doesn't flaunt her abilities.

One of our Golfwell Team followed Lydia at the New Zealand Open.

"Lydia drove off the first tee and hit it to the right into a fairway bunker. That wasn't the best way to start a tournament, I thought."

"Then, she casually walked down the first fairway quietly confident and totally unfazed."

"She walked into the bunker, studied her shot, selected the right club, ground her feet into the sand, and hit it three feet from the pin and birdied the first hole."

Lydia's recommends it's always best to keep your composure, "If I make a bogey or three putt, I'm on fire inside."

"But, it's not like you're going to play any better slamming your club or getting angry. So, you might as well just keep it in."

"People say I'm pretty calm, but I do make mistakes and I do get angry, but I try and not show it."

Lydia has great confidence. How did she first get it?

A pro who knew her very well and watched her progress over the years said, "Once she won the Canadian Open as an amateur, she knew then she could win playing against the very best."

"That win made her confident enough to take on anyone after winning against the best LPGA Players."

"She didn't get flustered," the pro added.

"And, it takes years to train yourself to keep calm," the pro added.

Lydia has a unique way of handling double bogeys. "The best cure for a double-bogey is a toffee, or sugar - any type of sugar; I love my chocolate."

Lydia believes you can't dwell on the past. Better to stay in the present.

Lydia has been focusing on her golf swing.

"It's important for me to understand more about my swing and my game, no matter who I end up working with."

"I feel like there are a lot of positives in my swing."

"I'm working on the rhythm of my swing, being able to keep my rhythm, and being more consistent."

"Consistency is what I'm looking for, performance-wise."

"Believe in yourself! Have faith in your abilities!"

"Without a humble but reasonable confidence in your own powers you cannot be successful or happy."

- Norman Vincent Peale

6. "CONCENTRATION COMES OUT OF A COMBINATION OF CONFIDENCE AND HUNGER." - Arnold Palmer

"He was a man who didn't change."

"It didn't matter if you cut the grass or you were a president."

"He was the same with everybody."

> *– Ernie Els*

Arnie had humble beginnings. "I grew up in poverty on the edge of a golf course."

"I saw how people lived on the other side of the tracks, the upper crust and the WASPs at the country club."

Arnie explained, "We had chickens and pigs in our yards. We butchered every year. I'll never forget those things."

Arnie was asked the best way to inspire young golfers interested in a professional golf career.

Arnie said, "First you have to have a desire to win."

"I can't be casual about losing," Arnie said. but dont get discourage when you do lose. "I always think I have a chance to win until winning is absolutely impossible."

Arnie has said, "The road to success is always under construction."

And he added, "You've got to keep working on your game.

"Young golfers need, concentration, confidence, competitive urge, and a large capacity for enjoyment."

As for concentration, Arnie explained, "The secret of concentration is the secret of self-discovery."

"You reach inside yourself to discover your personal resources, and what it takes to match them to the challenge."

And be persistent. "Always make a total effort, even when the odds are against you."

Arnie has said the greatest inspiration in his golf career was his father, Deacon "Deke" Palmer who worked his way up from ground maintenance at the Latrobe Country Club to the Club's resident golf pro. Deke was always tough on Arnie.

"He didn't want me to ever think golf would be an easy road. He was right. It hasn't been easy. Fun, but not easy."

"I couldn't understand why he wasn't throwing more accolades my way for all the great things I was doing."

Inspiring people by being tough on them sometimes has the opposite effect, but Arnie explained, "I know better now. He didn't want to puff me up too full of myself."

"My father said, 'Just remember something. You don't need to tell anybody how good you are. You show them how good you are.'"

Arnie added, "And he drove that home with me."

As a result of that, Arnie explained, "So, I learned early not to brag about how good I was or what I could do, and show them that I could play well enough."

Arnie's advice for young players is to always respect the game and maintain good manners in golf since golf is basically a gentleman's game.

"Sportsmanship is important, but keep in mind, I never rooted against an opponent, but I never rooted for him either."

In 2015, he told Tiger Woods the way to regain his golfing ability was to do two simple things: "Practice and have confidence."

Arnie said when your confidence level is low, one way to regain confidence is to "Find a golf instructor that you have confidence in."

And, he added, "If you can't find one, be your own coach."

The best players in Arnie's era were Nicklaus, Player, Ray Floyd, etc. Arnie explained, "They all had pros they worked with from time to time, but out on Tour, thousands of miles from home, each of them learned to be his own best coach."

Arnie also believed you don't have to be the physically strongest person.

"Success in this game depends less on strength of body than strength of mind and character."

And, Arnie never gave up. "I've always made a total effort, even when the odds seemed entirely against me."

And, "I never quit trying; I never felt that I didn't have a chance to win."

If confidence comes from practicing, Arnie spoke about the benefits of practicing. "The more I practice the luckier I get."

And, "I probably have a club in my hands 360 days a year, one way or another, playing with friends or just fiddling around or hitting balls."

One final thought from Arnie about knowing yourself and being a success.

"I can only tell you one thing that I do know for sure, I am a dreamer."

"There are not many people that will recognize or want to recognize the fact that they are dreamers in their own life," Arnie said.

"I get up in the morning, enthusiastically, and go pick up a golf club with a thought that I can somewhere find that secret to making the cut."

"That's just an example, but it applies to other things in life, too, and that's the way I live and the way I think and the way I feel."

"He (Arnold Palmer) had this other thing."

"It was the incredible ability to make you feel good - not just about him, but about yourself."

"I was amazed by how people reacted to him."

"He took energy from that and turned right around and gave it back."

– Tim Finchem, PGA Tour Commissioner

7. "TELLING ME I CAN'T DO SOMETHING IS THE WORST YOU CAN SAY TO ME, BECAUSE I'LL DEFINITELY DO IT. I'M VERY DETERMINED."

- Dustin Johnson

"The joke on Tour...it's funny, so many players, have gone up to DJ and we've all said, 'If we're playing golf the way you're playing golf, DJ, how could we not win?'"

- Padraig Harrington

Born in South Carolina, Dustin's father taught him the game and coached him. Dustin played and practiced regularly at the range in his teens. He then went on and played college golf.

"I played college golf at Coastal Carolina University and joined the Tour in 2007."

Dustin won one tournament in each of the first seven years he was on tour. The only other golfer to do that was Tiger Woods. Dustin keeps a positive attitude. "When I look at a golf course, I don't see trouble."

Instead, Justin said, "I see opportunities."

Dustin carefully has surveyed each course he plays and said, "It might have tight fairways or heavy rough or be super long—that's fine by me."

Dustin believes you have to look at a golf course that way since troubling holes may make a player defensive.

When Dustin comes across a tough hole, he has the confidence to enjoy the challenge rather than approach it timidly.

A timid approach to a tough hole can lead to trying to "steer" a tee shot which usually results in trouble.

"I don't know about you, but if my drive is going to find the junk, I'd rather be 50 yards closer to the hole," says Justin.

"If you want to play safe, that's fine, just be sure you're committed to it," says Dustin.

As an example of his positive attitude, Dustin described the 10th hole at Whistling Straights, "It has a bunker in the middle of the fairway that calls for a 290-yard carry."

Dustin explains "Catching the bunker is a sure bogey or possibly worse." Butch Harmon, Dustin's coach, told him to hit a four iron off the tee on that hole.

Dustin replied, "Nah, I'm just going to send it." Dustin later drove over the bunker and wound up with a birdie on the hole.

Dustin's advice on driving. "Grab your driver, think about the best tee shot you've ever hit, and send it."

If you watch Dustin in action, it's hard to tell if he's leading the tournament by 10 shots or needs one shot to make the cut. On good shots or bad shots his emotions are in check.

"Keeping emotions in check is great for consistency but it's also very intimidating to others," said Dustin.

Jon Rahm, talked about D.J., "It's amazing how he's able to keep cool the entire round,"

Jon went on to say, "It amazes me. Honestly, he doesn't really make mistakes."

"I think he's learned from what he's done in the past and he's embracing it now and that's why he's winning tournaments."

At Augusta, Dustin said, "I keep getting more comfortable on the golf course, You learn stuff every time you go around there. It's getting better."

If you looked up the words, "Quiet and Confident" in the dictionary, you would probably see a picture of D.J.

Dustin's advice to young golfers on putting is, "You know what makes you miss more putts than anything?"

His answer, "The fear of missing."

Dustin believes, "You need to think like NFL defensive backs do."

"If a back gets beat on a pass play, they just line up and get ready to stop the next one."

Feel is very important too. "To make the tough ones, you've got to trust your feel."

"After you read a putt, try to get a sense for the pace you'll need."

Dustin adds that once you've got a good idea of the feel, "Don't worry about body positions or too many details."

Dustin recommends you let your subconscious take over lining your body before you putt. "Your body will naturally adjust if you've studied and looked at your target."

At the time of writing this, Dustin is ranked as the number one player in the world and averages 316 yards off the tee.

"There is a difference between conceit and confidence."

"Conceit is bragging about yourself."

"Confidence means you believe you can get the job done."

> *- Johnny Unitas*

8. "WHEN YOU SEE THAT MANY PEOPLE WITH A SMILE ON THEIR FACE, THEN YOU KNOW YOU MUST BE DOING SOMETHING RIGHT," - Greg Norman

"There is no question that Greg was not only one of the best players - if not the best - in the world for a lengthy period, he was one of golf's most popular."

  - Jack Nicklaus

Greg Norman totalled 331 weeks ranked as the #1 golfer in the world (only Tiger Woods had more weeks at #1).

Greg made his competitive attitude clear to all when he said, "I always wanted to be the best I could be at whatever I did."

Most think being #1 is the goal for all competitive golfers.

Surprisingly, Greg said, "I didn't want to be the number one golfer in the world. I just wanted to be as good as I could be."

We wrote to Greg Norman about this and he replied to us,

"My goal was always to be the best I could be."

"If you think about it, there is a finality in reaching the top spot. Not only is it hard to get there, but you can't stay forever on that perch."

"But being the best you can be is infinite."

"There's always room to grow. There's always something new to learn."

"And, there's always something new to do."

Greg has gone on record about making himself better and better. He has said his success came from hard work,

"I worked hard, I pushed myself hard, and I probably even expected too much of myself."

Greg started golf late at the age of 15 when he began caddying for his mother, Toni, who herself won 18 Club championships.

Greg learned golf techniques from reading Jack Nicklaus' "Golf My Way," and absorbed himself in the book. He turned pro at 21. He wound up winning over 91 pro tournaments and 2 majors.

Greg's has gone on record with his advice to young golfers wanting to go on tour is, "You have to have it in your heart to work very hard at it."

"You should understand it's not an easy road as you experience successes and failures. Be determined to continue on the right path. Be aware set backs will happen."

"You take a step up and then you're knocked back two steps."

"So you got to get prepared mentally and physically for the ups and downs."

"You have to prepare yourself to give up a lot – your family and friends - since you are going to be dedicating 90% of the year, if not more, to the game of golf."

"You'll be giving up the rest of the things you enjoy in life while you pursue a career."

Greg has noticed there are plenty of good young golfers who are just as good as the players on tour.

"What you are searching for is that one moment where you clearly realize you are just as good as anyone else and you will get confident about your ability and that is what will keep you going."

"When you see people admiring your ability and smiling, know in your heart you've got the ability and focus on preparing your heart and mind to accomplish reaching that one moment when you truly realize you are just as good as anyone else."

9. "DAD WAS MY BEST FRIEND, ROLE MODEL, COACH, AND MENTOR." -Tiger Woods

"That's the easiest 65 I've ever seen in my life."

"From the second hole onwards, I thought, 'Hang on a minute."

"This is something extraordinary' This is a game that I had not seen before, and none of us had."

- Colin Montgomerie, playing with Tiger in the third-round commenting on Tiger's play at the 1997 Masters

Earl Woods introduced his son, Tiger, to golf before the age of 2.

"As a child, the family that I had, and the love I had from my two parents allowed me to go ahead and be more aggressive, to search and to take risks knowing that, if I failed, I could always come home to a family of love and support."

"One of the things that my parents have taught me is never listen to other people's expectations."

"You should live your own life and live up to your own expectations, and those are the only things I really care about it."

Some may say Earl might have forced Tiger into a golf career, but the reality was he didn't have to, as Tiger just simply enjoyed the game for itself.

"Don't force your kids into sports. I never was," said Tiger.

"To this day, my dad has never asked me to go play golf. I ask him."

"It's the child's desire to play that matters, not the parent's desire to have the child play."

Tiger added, "Fun. Keep it fun."

When he hit a bad shot, he kept a positive attitude.

"The only thing you can do is take a learning experience from it, positives and negatives, and apply them to the future."

Playing a bad first round at a tournament doesn't discourage Tiger.

"There are times when I just don't start off very well and it was a long day."

So what did Tiger think when he had a bad day?

"All day I was grinding away at the shots, but I stayed as patient as possible."

Tiger explained even if your first round goes bad, he feels, "I know I have three more days to get back into it."

"I will go home, relax and put this day behind me."

And, Tiger also pointed out sometimes things simply go right.

"It comes down to what you did right and what you did did wrong. And, some weeks I do a lot of things right."

And, Tiger adds, "I love to compete. That's the essence of who I am."

Golf can be like climbing a mountain that has no limit to its elevation. "No matter how good you get you can always get better and that's the exciting part," said Tiger.

Tiger worked very hard at golf. His golf teamate at Stanford, Notah Begay III, used to call Tiger, "Urkel", jokingly referring to the TV character, Steven Quincy Urkel, since Tiger had such a strong work ethic.

Tiger said, "People don't understand that when I grew up, I was never the most talented. I was never the biggest. I was never the fastest. I certainly was never the strongest."

"The only thing I had was my work ethic, and that's been what has gotten me this far."

"That's why I've busted my butt on the range for hours on end and made changes to get to this point where I'm able to compete at the highest level in major championships. That's where you want to be."

Tiger's practice sessions are lengthy up to 7-8 hours per day. "I hit various shots and practice with all clubs. I shape shots and keep range work interesting. Then, I practice putting on the practice green."

Then he spends the afternoon hours on the course working on his swing and practicing his short game.

Tiger used his imagination when he trained as a kid.

"As a kid, I might have been psycho, I guess, but I used to throw golf balls in the trees and try and somehow make par from them. I thought that was fun."

And, it's not the money that drives Tiger. "If money titles meant anything, I'd play more tournaments."

"The only thing that means a lot to me is winning."

Tiger explains, "If I have more wins than anybody else and win more majors than anybody else in the same year, then it's been a good year."

Tiger adds, "I wake up every day and I can't wait to go to work, and that's a gift. Not too many people have the opportunity to feel that way."

Tiger maintains a positive winning attitude in golf competitions, "There's no sense in going to a tournament if you don't believe that you can win it. And that is the attitude I have always had. And that is not going to change."

"I mean, as an athlete, as a competitor, you have to have that belief in yourself."

Tiger has a strong desire to win majors. But he's shared what motivates him more.

"The joy I get from winning a major championship doesn't even compare to the feeling I get when a kid writes a letter saying: 'Thank you so much. You have changed my life.'"

"I love to compete. That's the essence of who I am."

-Tiger Woods

10. "THERE'S NO SUCH THING AS A NATURAL TOUCH. TOUCH IS SOMETHING YOU CREATE BY HITTING MILLIONS OF GOLF BALLS," - Lee Trevino

"Every day is April Fool's Day to my friend, Lee Trevino."

- Jack Nicklaus

Lee Trevino has an unorthodox, self-taught swing:

"I'll take a golf lesson when I find an instructor who can beat me," Lee has said.

He was raised by his mother and grandfather in a poor home without electricity or plumbing.

By the age of 8, he found work caddying at the Glen Lakes Country Club. Lee was influenced by the fact there was money to made at golf. So, he quit school after 8th grade, and worked at the driving range and hit hundreds of balls a day as a teenager.

His hard work paid off and he was inducted into the World Golf Hall of Fame in 1981. He won several majors and his wit and charm made the "Merry Mex" a favorite with the fans.

At the 1971 U.S. Open, Lee was in an 18 hole playoff against Jack Nicklaus at Merion Golf Club.

There was a lot of tension in the air as they were about to tee off on the first tee. Lee looked around sensing the tension in the air. So what does he do?

Lee pulled out a long rubber snake from his golf bag and dangled it for the crowd. It was April Fool's Day as well.

Jack, sitting down and waiting to get started, asked to see it. Lee happily tossed it over Jack and everyone had a good laugh releasing some of the tension. Lee went on to win the 18-hole playoff.

Racism didn't bother Lee. "Sure, I've felt racism. I think everybody has prejudice."

"When I was growing up, the dark Mexican kids weren't allowed in the public swimming pool in Dallas. My light-skinned friend got in, and he laughed at us."

"It didn't seem like a big deal, because we didn't know any different. So, I never ran into anything that actually scared me."

He kept a witty and relaxed attitude when he played competitions and had many well-known quips like, "Pressure is when you play for five dollars a hole - with only two dollars in your pocket."

Or, "In case of a thunderstorm, stand in the middle of the fairway and hold up a one iron. Not even God can hit a one iron."

Lee was hit by lightning several times on the golf course and joked about it often. "How can they beat me? I've been struck by lightning, had two back operations, and been divorced twice."

Lee was a determined player. "I'm not out there just to be dancing around. I expect to win every time I tee up."

After he retired from the PGA Tour, he had a very successful career on the Senior (Champions) Tour.

Lee advises young players to occasionally practice playing with one club.

"Playing matches with one club is the best way to learn to play the game."

"If you're allowed only one club you have to create a tremendous number of shots with it."

"It's the best way for youngsters to learn finesse around the course and to develop a tremendous feel around the green," says Lee.

> *"I'm not out there just to be dancing around. I expect to win every time I tee up."*
>
> *- Lee Trevino*

11. "CONFIDENCE IS THE MOST IMPORTANT SINGLE FACTOR IN THIS GAME," says Jack Nicklaus

"Jack knew he was going to beat you. You knew Jack was going to beat you."

"And Jack knew that you knew that he was going to beat you."

> *-Tom Weiskopf*

Jack has said, "No matter how great your natural talent, there is only one way to obtain and sustain confidence: hard work."

Moreover, Jack said, "Nobody - but nobody - has ever become really proficient at golf without practice, without doing a lot of thinking and then hitting a lot of shots."

"It isn't so much a lack of talent; it's a lack of being able to repeat good shots consistently that frustrates most players. And the only answer to that is practice," says Jack.

Even if there are many others who look like they have natural talent, Jack said, "Talent isn't as important as the work and dedication necessary to become competent."

Jack says to forget about your competitors and think about the course. "Once you play a tournament, you're playing against the golf course, you're playing against yourself and trying to do the best you can."

Jack points out it's important to believe and trust in yourself and what you want to do in life.

"Pursue what you love, what you are passionate about. Don't let somebody else dictate your life's path."

No matter what you go through, don't get down on yourself. Jack said, "You've got to want to be the best golfer the world has ever seen."

Jack's advice for young golfers. "Quit trying to play "hero" shots from severe trouble situations... All that does is compound small errors into large disasters."

As far as your competitors go, Jack said this about winning and losing.

"Some people sometimes say it's OK to lose if your opponent has a hot round."

But, Jack says to forget that.

"I hate to lose -- period."

So, what does Jack think if he is losing before starting a round? "If a guy is going to shoot a 10 under par, I am going to shoot an 11 under par."

"Sometimes the biggest problem is in your head."

So, what do you do to shake the bad thoughts out of your head?

Jack said, "You've got to believe you can play a shot instead of wondering where your next bad shot is coming from."

Jack strongly believes you have to have confidence and believe in yourself. As an amateur, Jack said, "I expected to win every tournament I entered. If I didn't, I was a bum."

Jack believes there's nothing wrong with winning.

"I liked being top man," said Jack.

Johnny Miller said,

"When Nicklaus plays wells well, he wins."

"When he plays badly, he finishes second."

"And, when he plays terribly, he finishes third,"

"You've got to have the confidence that you can win; you've got to expect to win,' said Jack.

Yes, but what if you don't expect to win?

Jack's answer was very simple, "If you don't expect to win, you have no business being there."

But, Jack points out it's important to have realistic expectations.

"Achievement is largely the product of steadily raising one's level of aspiration and expectation."

So, it's a gradual process of reaching one plateau of confidence and skill after another in order to achieve. You just don't get there overnight.

But, being tired sometimes will hurt you.

"Being tired will not show up first when you hit full shots," said Jack.

Jack added, "Unless you are very, very tired, you will be able to hit full shots just as solidly as ever."

"When tiredness strikes, the first effect is on the delicate shots in and around the green that require so much concentration."

"A tired player can't concentrate, he completely loses his sense of 'feel.'"

Jack said confidence comes with practice and he used to practice in a very unique way (which probably made him one of the best long iron players).

"Quite often when I am preparing to play a tournament at an extremely long course, I will go out with an 8-to-10 handicapper at home in Columbus and hit his second shots."

Jack does this so he is, "forced to play a lot of long irons, many of them from difficult angles into the green."

Jack has said becoming a great golfer is like becoming a great doctor.

"So many of these fellas think they can come right out of college and make a living in pro golf. Look, we're not much different from doctors."

"A young doctor doesn't expect to do open-heart surgery the day he graduates from medical school."

Jack explains you've got to be ready to do the job.

"The doctor has to spend so many years learning, and he's hungry and maybe broke during that time. The doctor doesn't begin to make it until he's really ready to do a job. It's the same with the pro golfer."

Jack said, having confidence does a very interesting thing to the mind when you're under pressure. "Pressure is what you live for...if you are going to be successful in life, you're going to have pressure."

"The biggest tension-reliever of all in golf is confidence."

"Concentration blocks out pressure. If you make mistakes and look for excuses, you lose your concentration and feel pressure. I try to keep from doing that."

Jack has a single swing thought in pressure situations too. "One thought is especially helpful in combating pressure."

"The one thought that has been the most beneficial over the years to me is, interestingly enough, also the simplest. The thought is: complete the backswing."

Jack said, "I made mistakes in my early years on Tour, and if I would have corrected those, I would have won several more majors."

He says he lost a U.S. Open to Lee Trevino by leaving shot in the bunker after trying to hit a low percentage shot out of the bunker. After that he didn't ever again try to get fancy with a bunker shot.

Jack, who has finished second 19 times in major golf tournaments and finished in the top three 46 times, says losing does have its benefits.

"Near misses in majors are part of the learning process. Tom Watson went through that. Rory

McIlroy went through that—you blow a couple of majors, but you learn how to win."

So, per Jack, you've got to go through the good and bad when learning the game. "I wouldn't want to trade it, because the learning process is so valuable."

Jack Grout was the first and only coach for Jack and started coaching him when Jack was 10 years old.

"Jack Grout knew the golf swing probably as well as any instructor ever has," said Jack.

"But I think his greatest gift to his students was his belief in them and his ability to get them to believe in themselves."

"He wanted you not only to be skilled technically, but also to be so confident of your skills that you could identify and fix your own swing flaws even in the heat of battle, even without him there by your side."

"In other words, Jack Grout worked to be dispensable. He wanted his students to be able to function at the highest level without him."

12. "GOING TO THE GYM IS GREAT FOR YOUR BODY, BUT IT'S ALSO GREAT FOR YOUR MIND," said Rory McIlroy.

"A static golfer has to hit each shot perfectly to win."

"Rory says, 'I don't have to play perfect, I don't have to hit each shot perfectly.'"

"'If I have to chip or scrap my way to win, I'll do it.'"

"Scrapping your way to win is the sign of a dynamic golfer vs. a static golfer."

"Rory is a dynamic golfer."

- Dr. Gio Valente talking about Rory McIroy

"My parents inspired and encouraged me to have a golf career," said Rory.

Rory's dad coached him from a very young age.

"My mom and dad worked very hard to give me the best chance in - not just in golf but in life."

"You know, I was an only child, you know, my dad worked three jobs at one stage. My mom worked night shifts in a factory."

His father, Gerry said, "Sometimes, you might get a bit browned off or tired but Rosie would always cheer me up. 'Gerry,' she'd say, 'One day this could be all worthwhile'.

Gerry said, "We wanted to give Rory a chance at a golf career."

And he added, "After all, he was the only one we have."

Hi parents didn't force Rory one bit, "Golf was not our dream, it was Rory's.'"

Rory explains one of the reasons he plays well is, "My dad's a scratch golfer and I've got the knack of seeing something and then replicating it."

"I saw my dad swing a club and I worked out how to do the same thing."

Has Rory changed his swing? He's said, "My backswing and follow-through have been basically the same since I was two."

And, Rory doesn't forget what his parents did for him. "I wanted to make a point of basing myself at home, being close to my family."

"I'll never be able to repay Mum and Dad for what they did, but at least they know they'll never have to work another day. I'll do whatever it takes to look after them."

At the 2017 Bay Hill Classic, Rory shared a letter he received from Arnold Palmer in 2011.

Palmer told Rory he was, "In a position where you have the opportunity to give back to the game that is making you famous and I hope, and certainly feel sure, that you will live up to that obligation in the months and years ahead."

Palmer then told Rory to, "Just continue to be yourself. Don't change."

Rory is giving back to the game, especially to young golfers. "Being yourself is important," said Rory. "To be a top-class athlete, you have to train hard, you have to eat right, you have to get enough rest. I feel the way golf is going nowadays, you have to treat yourself as an athlete."

The right diet is important to young golfers. "If I'm playing in the morning, I'll get some carbs early: porridge with chopped banana."

"If I'm playing in the afternoon, I'll start with less carbs and have some eggs and fruit for breakfast, then a light lunch about 90 minutes before I play, so I don't feel sluggish or full."

But depending on the starting times, "I sometimes eat a little sandwich or a slow-release energy bar - one on the front nine and one on the back nine"

"You're out there five hours, so you have to keep eating. You're going to burn at least 1,000 calories. I'll try to take in about 400-600 calories during a round and drink water."□

Rory also believes driving the golf ball is very important and recommends widening your stance and place your weight on the insides of your feet and both arches. "This helps balance you and allows you to turn your hips and use your legs more."

"I keep my left foot turned slightly out and do a wide takeaway and take my time transitioning from the top."

Rory continues, "Rushing my downswing has been a problem for me (and other young golfers) at times, so I stay relaxed and balanced and do a smooth transition with a nice even tempo."

"Tempo will help you strike the ball better no matter what kind of shot making you're doing," says Rory.

His thoughts on confidence and your presence on the course are, "You know I need that cockiness, the self-belief, arrogance, swagger, whatever you want to call it, I need that on the golf course to bring the best out of myself."

But when he's not competing, he's different. "Once I leave the golf course, you know that all gets left there."

And he leaves it there. "The great thing about my two lives is I love them both."

"I'm very ambitious and nothing gets in the way of me practicing and concentrating on winning golf tournaments. But then I come home and get back to normality."

Rory agrees not to ever let your competitors see you sweat.

"I mean I don't want to feel inferior to any other golfer in the world."

"You know if you do that, then you know you're giving them an advantage, you know, right from the start."

Rory believes you shouldn't be concerned about beating a rival.

"I've always said the players don't build up rivalries themselves, people from the outside build up the rivalries"

"I just want to play good golf. I want to try and keep winning golf tournaments."

"All you need in this life is ignorance and confidence, and then success is sure."

- Mark Twain

(What Mark Twain meant was, learn to conquer the enemy within and ignore any self-doubt. Don't let your negative thoughts work against you.)

13. "WE CREATE SUCCESS OR FAILURE ON THE COURSE PRIMARILY BY OUR THOUGHTS." - Gary Player

Gary Player ranks third in the number of total tournaments won behind Robert De Vincenzo and Sam Snead. He's won all four major championships.

He began playing golf in South Africa at the age of 14 when his father who worked in the mines got a loan to buy his son a set of clubs.

Gary played his first round of golf at the Virginia Park Golf Course in Johannesburg and parred the first three holes he ever played. But, Gary adds, "I'm not a 'natural' at it.'

A career playing competitive golf isn't glamorous. Gary said, "I've lived in motels for 63 years, being away from my family and country, my farm, and made a lot of sacrifices to become a world champion."

But Gary adds, "I learned that the dedication and the sacrifices and what I went through is worth it."

"It was tough on my wife. I tell my wife every day how much I love her."

Gary did that unconditionally. "And I keep telling her how beautiful she is, even if she wasn't."

"Beauty is in the eye of the beholder, and you've got to work at your marriage."

Gary is the first to admit there is no set pattern to playing well.

"Golf is a puzzle without an answer." Gary said.

He added, "I've played the game for 40 years and I still haven't the slightest idea how to play."

Gary Player is over 80 years old. "You have to realize your body is a holy temple, and you have to be in shape for longevity, for productivity, and to excel and to be able to contribute to society."

You are what you eat and he adds, "Stay away from all of these kook diets. It's not DIE-it, but it's LIVE-it. It's simple."

So, what does Gary recommend for a diet? "Eat half of the amount you eat now. Cut out the high fats. and the high sugars. And exercise 3-4 times per week."

Gary's advice for young golfers is straight forward and unique.

"Appreciate America. Work hard. Realize everybody has problems. Take advantage of the opportunity you have."

He adds, "Don't dream about doing well, do it, and remember, the Chinese and Koreans are outworking us."

Finally, Gary, along with most others, believe there is no such thing as a person who has a natural ability to play golf, i.e. a "natural golfer." "You must work very hard to become a natural golfer."

14. "PRACTICE BUILDING UP YOUR SWING SPEED AND YOUR SHORT GAME," - Rickie Fowler

Photo courtesy of Jeff Farsai, Long Beach, CA

Rickie's Dad and Mom taught him to be humble and to let his golf do the talking.

Rickie began learning to play golf at an early age.

"My grandpa was the one; he started taking up golf when I was about two and introduced me to the game."

"He just took me to the driving range where I grew up playing."

"That was really all he had to do was let me hit a golf ball and kind of fell in love with it from there."

"He didn't really have to teach me a whole lot or anything."

Later, Barry McDonnell, a golf pro, taught Rickie the fundamental "old school" golf swing. "We started working together when I was 7," said Rickie.

Rickie wasn't given a large amount of detailed instruction. "We'd go to the end of the range, he'd smoke his cigar, and I'd be hitting away."

Rickie explained, "We never laid sticks on the ground for alignment, and we never used a video camera - I don't think he knew how to operate one."

Rickie said Barry taught him the fundamental golf swing and how to align the clubface and worked on ball flight, "and making sure the ball was starting where I wanted it to." Barry made shot making interesting to Rickie vs. just hitting one ball after another which gets tedious.

And Rickie loved the game. "I spent years on the range while I was growing up," said Rickie.

"Many young golfers are too quick with their backswing," says Rickie.

"When I need a drive on the fairway going into the final holes, I think only about making a slow and deliberate backswing and not to be too quick at the top."

"Beginning with a slow and deliberate backswing, makes it easier to make a smooth transition."

"One of my tendencies is to be too quick on the downswing and the club gets behind me and the ball could go anywhere."

Rickie also recommends to pick a small target of where you want the drive to go and where you want the ball to start out at.

"Sometimes I have a loop at the top of my swing."

The loop originated from using his Dad's 43.5-inch shafted driver which wasn't cut down to kid size.

"I've worked with Butch Harmon on taking the loop out - to just bring the club back on the same line."

When Rickie played the Ryder Cup with Jimmy Walker, they both looked at the first hole and Jimmy was thinking three wood off the tee.

"Jimmy hit three wood, but I felt more confident and comfortable with driver."

"Be confident with your driver. It's got a big face and a big sweet spot. Tee it up and let it go."

Rickie explained when he is hitting the ball well, he doesn't hit any other club straighter than his driver.

Rickie's advice to young golfers looking for a career in golf is to practice hitting the ball hard and straight.

"As you are growing up and taking up the game, work on developing your speed up."

Rickie feels distance is an advantage. "There's so much of an advantage you have, when can hit it long, and with longer distances involved in the game, that's a plus now."

"On the flip side of the coin is the short game and you have to practice and be confident in your short game."

15. "MY ONLY GOAL IS TO LOOK BACK EACH YEAR AND SEE IF I'VE IMPROVED." – Jim Furyk

"Jim is a solid, dogged competitor with a great short game."

"He's made himself into a great player and he's not going to go away."

"Whatever you think of his swing, it repeats itself well, time and time again, and time and time again under pressure."

> *-Tom Lehman*

Mike Furyk, an assistant golf pro, taught his son, Jim to play golf in the Pittsburg area as he grew up. "I played basketball in high school and also played golf."

He played College Golf at the University of Arizona. He shot a 58 in 2016, the lowest score ever in a PGA Tour event.

PGA of American President Paul Levy announced,

""For more than two decades, Jim Furyk has stood proud and tall on the American golf stage and we are thrilled to have him as our Ryder Cup Captain for 2018."

Mr. Levy added, "He's got inherent competitive spirit and leadership traits…and is well suited for the task at hand. He's played in 9 consecutive Ryder Cups."

Jim has a lot of Ryder Cup experience and will be the Club Captain for the 2018 Ryder Cup.

"We tend to tighten up as a whole during the Ryder Cup."

Jim adds, "I think you can just take a look at the guys' faces in the locker room and on the bus. …"

And, Jim said, "Everyone just looks a little bit more uptight during Ryder Cup week."

If you're playing in an individual tournament, Jim said don't let a bad start get to you.

"There's times when you can get off to a bad start, look up on the board and see guys getting off to a good start."

Jim says you must fight your competitive urges. "You want to go out and try to force things and try to make some birdies."

But Jim says it's best to stay with it. "I stayed patient and just let it happen."

For example, let's say you're playing the first round and things are going medium.

Jim said this. "You get off the first day and you're even through six and you want to start trying to push. You have to let things happen. If you force it and try to make those things happen, I think that's when the course jumps up and bites you."

But Jim says, don't be timid. "I don't think you want to play cautiously because that means you're playing scared."

"You have to play aggressive but *intelligent*."

Having good sportsmanship will help you, Jim said. "Ultimately, you try not to let the other guys affect how you're playing, but it's nice to see a friend having a good day. And I think it helps you a little bit."

Don't be too concerned about length, Jim said.

Don't put too much emphasis on length.

Jim said, "Do I wish I was longer?"

"Sure. I'll get longer, but everybody else will, too."

Jim explained, "It was a power game last year, and I finished fourth on the money list, so it can be done."

"Work like you don't need the money. Love like you've never been hurt. Dance like nobody's watching."

- Satchel Paige

16. "YOU'VE GOT TO FEEL GOOD ABOUT YOURSELF," says Bubba Watson

"I think he's such a great role model for golf and for sports in general because he's real, he's authentic, and he's someone who doesn't care what other people think."

> *-Tim Tebow*

Bubba Watson was given a cut down 9 iron by his father when he was 6 years old and for hours, Bubba hit plastic whiffle golf balls with it.

"My good father gave me a lesson and I practiced and practiced."

"Instead of playing with army men or whatever, I played golf, like for hours every day," said Bubba.

His father influenced him the most.

"My dad - who was a tough guy, a Green Beret - always looked nice and wore these bright Sansa belt pants."

Bubba remembers his dad always said, "You have two options: You can be a follower or you can be a leader."

His father added, "And you don't ever want to follow anybody."

"And that's kind of become my philosophy about everything." Bubba said.

Bubba added, "He didn't discipline me too hard when I was growing up, but he was persistent about having me always getting better."

Today, Bubba has a great deal of confidence in his game. "What I say goes. I'm hitting shots that I want to hit."

And, he adds, "I'm doing the things that I want to do. I play it my way."

He played for the University of Georgia before he turned pro.

He keeps positive about his shot making. "If I have a swing, I have a shot."

Bubba has made mistakes. And, he learns from his mistakes.

"When I make mistakes, when your friends call you out, when the media calls you out, when my wife calls me out, when my mom calls me out...."

Bubba added, "When these people call you out and tell you you're doing something wrong, it's not to punish you or get on to you."

"It's about to help you improve later in life," says Bubba.

"That's the only way I'm going to improve ... to get better as a person."

"It's important to feel good about yourself," said Bubba.

Bubba said mistakes are important since, "That's how you become a better man.... I bet sometime before I pass away, unless I pass away tonight, I'm going to mess up again."

Bubba says it's important to just be yourself.

"I don't play the sport for fame. I don't try to win tournaments for fame. I don't do any of that. It's just me. I'm just Bubba. I goof around. I joke around. I just want to be me and play golf."

He adds, "I'm not afraid of anything. My two favorite colors are lime green and hot pink. (he has a hot pink driver). I mean, I really like pink. And I don't care who knows it. I'm already married, sooo..."

"Beauty is when you can appreciate yourself. When you love yourself, that's when you're most beautiful."

- Zoe Kravitz

17. "DON'T SWING YOUR DRIVER VIOLENTLY OR RUSH IT AT THE END." - Phil Mickleson

"I think one day, he might be asked to be a captain."

"He understands what it takes… He's had the experience. He's had the bad and the good."

"When he speaks, everybody listens. He's earned that respect because of the game of golf and his history, what he's done for the game of golf."

-Bubba Watson on Phil Mickleson

Phil started playing golf at the age of 3 and would run off by himself to the golf course not telling his parents.

His mother said, "Sometimes, he told neighbors he was going to the golf course on his way there."

David Feherty said, "Phil is brilliant, but he's nuts. There's something not quite right about that boy."

"Phil is watching a movie that only Phil can see."

"His mother told me, 'Phil was so clumsy as a little boy, we had to put a football helmet on him until he was 4 because he kept bumping into things.'"

"I told her, 'Mary, Mary, I'm a writer, you can't keep handing me material like this.'"

"So, the next time I saw Phil I said, 'You didn't really wear a football helmet in the house until you were 4, did you?'"

"He said, 'It was more like 5.'"

Phil is a fierce competitor and has said, "The object of golf is not just to win. It is to play like a gentleman, and win."

Phil won tournaments in his teens (three times an American Junior Golf award winner), and because of his success in Junior Golf, he received a full scholarship at Arizona State.

He graduated and had a remarkable NCAA career. "I won three NCAA individual championships, three Haskins Awards for outstanding collegiate golfer, and received First Team All-American honors all four years."

He then turned pro.

Phil's advice for up and coming golfers (as well as weekend golfers) is, "Don't try to be something different from what you are, but don't be afraid to try new things especially in your short game."

"Make sure you practice your short game, that's where you'll save strokes," says Phil.

And Phil wants to make it clear to young players, "The only way to win tournaments is with the short game."

Chipping and pitching are extremely important. Phil said, "Over half your shots out here are within 30 or 40 yards."

And, use the right golf ball. "Use the best golf ball you can find to give you the best distance off your driver, while at the same time find a ball which allows you spin and control for your short game."

Phil said you do this by "Trying different balls until you find the one."

On your golf swing, Phil has said, "Don't try to have a quick and violent swing. It takes a toll on your body. I haven't had a serious injury during 23 years on tour."

Phil says it best to "Build your speed up gradually with your driver instead of violently swinging or trying to kill the ball."

"And, don't rush your swing right as you are about to hit the ball."

If you plan a career in golf, staying healthy is very important.

Finally, Phil points out to young golfers, "Remember you are learning. Keep positive, you will gain knowledge and experience in each competition."

18. "TRAIN TO BE CONSISTENT IN YOUR FUNDAMENTALS." - Adam Scott

"Everybody questioned whether he could do it. We all knew it. The players know it. I think he'll go on and win more majors than any other Australian golfer."

> *- Greg Norman*

Adam practices very hard, "Golf is all-consuming for me. I'm constantly thinking about improving and how I'm going to do better, even when I'm doing well I'm trying to do better and better all the time,"

Adam Scott was the first Australian golfer to win the Masters (Greg Norman came close very close to winning the Masters by finishing second on three occasions).

Adam began playing golf at the age of 4. He was coached by his father. Adam practiced and played throughout childhood and his teen years.

His father, a PGA Club pro, said he tried to teach Adam only the fundamentals of golf not wanting "to crowd his mind with too many technical thoughts."

Fundamentals are certainly important as John Updike said, "The golf swing is like a suitcase into which we are trying to pack one too many things."

Adam loved the game and began beating his father when Adam reached 13 years of age.

Adam later played college golf at UNLV. He then went pro and won on the European Tour and then joined the PGA Tour and continued winning.

Adam later broke his hand and wasn't playing well.

Adam said, ""We've seen it so many times with different players. You think you're on top of things and then all of a sudden you feel like you are at rock bottom, or heading that way anyway."

Adam went on to say, "At some point, you have to right the ship, or you keep going backwards."

"I guess it wasn't at the rock-bottom point, since I started to see some improvement in my game."

"When you see some improvement, the hunger can kick in, and that makes the workload easier."

"Winning is not easy. Sometimes you need to stick it out, fight hard and not implode."

Adam's advice to junior golfers is to focus on your fundamentals. "Have a good pre-shot routine making sure your grip, stance and posture are correct."

"Have your coach check your fundamentals regularly so you don't fall into bad habits."

"Train to be as consistent as you can with the fundamentals," says Adam.

19. "THINK IT'S NOT WHAT YOU ACCOMPLISH IN LIFE, BUT WHAT YOU OVERCOME." - Johnny Miller

"The two most treasured analysts we have in sport are John McEnroe and Johnny Miller because they are so candid."

"No filter, no filter at all. Miller sees it and it goes right to his mouth and says it."

"He sees the game and obviously understands it brilliantly, but sees it better than anyone I've been able to observe."

-Dick Enberg

Johnny Miller starred at golf from an early age and won the 1964 US Junior Golf Championship.

He placed eighth as an amateur in the 1966 US Open. His confidence kept growing.

Lee Trevino commented about Johnny at 1966 U.S. Open:

"It was my first Open and I was running scared. But Johnny had some swagger, and he was already so good, it was like his forehead was stamped 'can't miss,'" said Lee.

Johnny won at total of 25 PGA Tour events including the 1973 US Open by shooting 63 in the final round on the tough narrow fairways at Oakmont Country Club. Three years later he won the British Open.

Johnny said, "In 1974, I won eight tournaments, the money title and the Player of the Year award and then won four more times in 1975." Johnny was referred to as the "Golden Boy" by the media.

Then, he went into a slump.

Johnny said, "I considered quitting professional golf during my slump several times between 1977 and 1979."

"But Jack Nicklaus supported and inspired me and helped me out of the slow year slumps."

"Jack showed me I didn't value enough what it was to be a champion. I didn't buy into the majors as much as I should have," said Johnny.

"During my slump, I had taken to reading the Scriptures a good bit as well as a few pieces on philosophy and life."

"I remember reading, 'It's not what you accomplish in life, but what you overcome.'"

"That inspired me and haunted me more than anything else."

Johnny added, "There was the one side of me that said, 'Let's quit,' and the other side that kept asking, 'What have you overcome?'"

"I kept thinking I've never climbed any mountains."

Johnny thought, "I've worked hard and ridden the crest of the waves all these years."

The Johnny realized, "But it all came relatively easy."

Johnny said to himself, "I never experienced anything like this slump. I refuse to let it get the better of me. I cannot give up."

Several years went by, then Johnny started to win again in 1980.

"I won 7 more PGA Tournaments including two AT&T Pebble Beach National Pro-Am Championships.

Lee Trevino played with Johnny Miller and many other golfing greats and also said this about Johnny,

"Johnny had that extremely weak grip like Hogan, and he would set it going back and then just release it as hard as he could with total confidence."

"He didn't have to re-route it or hold onto it or practice like hell, like most of the rest of us."

"Maybe because he grooved it so young, he was basically on automatic, where hitting the ball hard and straight and solid was actually easy."

"He got to a very rare place."

Finally, Lanny Wadkins, said this about Johnny Miller which is very helpful to young players to learn why Johnny had an amazing winning streak:

"Johnny was the best I ever saw at hitting pure golf shots."

"I was very fortunate to play with a lot of the true greats: Jack and Trevino and Tiger, sure, but also Snead, Hogan and Nelson, who might have been past it, but not so you couldn't see what they could do."

"But I can't imagine that anyone in history has ever consistently hit the ball as solid and as close to the pin as Johnny did."

"He could certainly work the ball, but his money shot was right at the flag with no curve, and 3-wood through wedge, the ball would never leave the flag."

"He had a technique and a sense for returning the clubface to absolutely dead square that was uncanny."

"The boy who is going to make a great man must not make up his mind merely to overcome a thousand obstacles,"

"He must make up his mind to win in spite of a thousand repulses and defeats."

- Theodore Roosevelt

20. "I COULD MAKE A PRETTY FAIR APPRAISAL OF THE WORTH OF AN OPPONENT BY TAKING A GOOD MEASURING LOOK INTO HIS EYES." -Bobby Jones

"Bob Jones, my first golf hero, once commented that he never learned anything from a golf tournament he won."

> *-Arnold Palmer*

Bobby Jones had health issues when he was a very young, so his doctor recommended he take up golf to build his strength. He took it up.

Bobby was coached by golf pros at an early age.

Jim Barnes, who won the 1921 US Open, watched Bobby play and said, "Bobby occasionally threw clubs as a teenager."

"That happens to an emotional teenager," Jim added.

And then he said, "Never mind the club-throwing and the beatings he's taking. Defeat will make him great. He's not satisfied now with a pretty good shot. He has to be perfect. That's the way a good artist must feel."

Bobby said, "I'm a perfectionist at golf." He developed a smooth - almost perfect golf swing.

Yet, golf puzzled him despite his creativity with shot making.

"There are times, when I feel that I know less about what I'm doing on a golf course than anyone else in the world," said Bobby.

He also said, "It is nothing new or original to say that golf is played one stroke at a time. But it took me many years to realize it."

Bobby's "One stroke at time quote" is something to ponder when you're trying to score a good round.

He was known to worry in competition. Historians report, "Bobby's stomach would get upset and he would eat lightly before a match, like toast with tea."

His famous quote, "Competitive golf is played mainly on a five-and-a-half-inch course... the space between your ears," is well understood by all golfers and great advice for keeping your cool on the course.

Before a match, Bobby would size up opponents by confidently looking into their eyes.

"I had held a notion that I could make a pretty fair appraisal of the worth of an opponent simply by speaking to him on the first tee and taking a good measuring look into his eyes."

Bobby knew he was worried too much about an opponent when he played match play.

"The object of golf is to beat someone. Make sure that someone is not yourself."

So, he forced himself to forget about who he was playing against and played against the course seeking pars or better on each hole.

"The toughest opponent of all is Old Man Par."

"Old Man Par is a patient soul who never shoots a birdie and never incurs a bogey."

And Bobby added, "If you travel the long road with him, you must be patient, too."

Staying in the present and clearing his mind from worry made it easier to play a course.

Bobby said, "A leading difficulty with the average player is that he totally misunderstands what is meant by concentration."

"He may think he is concentrating hard when he is merely worrying."

Concentration is staying in the present and dealing with the shot without any thoughts of a good or bad outcome.

Bobby learned patience and totally disregarded what his opponents were doing. He said, "When I take the attitude of playing for pars, I started to win matches more easily."

"No-one will ever have golf under his thumb."

That statement challenged many. Bobby added, "No round ever will be so good it could not have been better. Perhaps this is why golf is the greatest of games."

"You are not playing a human adversary; you a playing a game. You are playing old man par."

At the US Open at Winged Foot Golf Club in 1929 Bobby made a sloping, side hill putt on the 18th green to tie the leader, Al Espinosa.

That putt automatically raised Bobby's confidence. He beat Espinosa in a 36-hole playoff by 23 strokes.

Bobby was an excellent putter using a single blade putter he named, "Calamity Jane."

Over the years, Bobby, a lawyer by profession, developed his priorities, "First come my wife and children. Next comes my profession--the law. Finally, and never as a life in itself, comes golf."

His health deteriorated after he retired from golf. He compared golf to life by saying, "Golf is the closest game to the game we call life."

He explained, "You get bad breaks from good shots; you get good breaks from bad shots - but you have to play the ball where it lies."

"The main idea in golf as in life, I suppose is to learn to accept what cannot be altered and to keep on doing one's own reasoned and resolute best whether the prospect be bleak or rosy."

As for young golfers, Bobby said, "I get as much fun as the next man from whaling the ball as hard as I can and catching it squarely on the button."

When you're a young golfer, it's thrilling to hit a ball far. But Bobby explained, "From sad experience over the years, I learned not to try hitting it far in a round that meant anything."

Among his many records, Bobby Jones is the only player ever to have won the Grand Slam (pre-Masters) as it was known in his time by winning the following four major championship in 1930: 1) The Amateur Championship at the Old Course at St Andrews, Scotland. 2) The Open Championship at Royal Liverpool Golf Club. 3)The U.S. Open, at Interlachen Country Club, in Minnesota, and, 4) the U.S. Amateur, at Merion Golf Club, Pennsylvania.

21. "I ALWAYS BELIEVED WHEN YOU ENTER AN EVENT YOU GO OUT AND TRY TO WIN," said Patrick Reed.

"It's about sticking the knife in. Instead of just playing the match for the match."

"Jordan Spieth complimenting Patrick Reed on leading the US to Ryder Cup Victory."

"When I was younger I'd played in an upper age group, and early on learned how to get my butt kicked."

Patrick added, "When you're young and doing that, you watch older guys hit the ball so much farther."

But Patrick didn't give up. "As I got older, the more I started to win, the more I boosted my confidence. I knew I can compete."

Several years ago, Patrick said (just trying to be honest), he sincerely felt he was one the top five players in the world. He got a lot of criticism for that.

"I just try to be honest and say what I believe. Sometimes it gets me in trouble and sometimes it doesn't."

Patrick added, "All I could do was work on my game to get more consistent and get back to the winner's circle."

We certainly agree with that attitude as hard work gets your mind off unnecessary worries.

"I've learned from it, too. I felt like the whole "Top 5" comment got spun a little bit."

So, how does Patrick build and maintain his confidence?

"I set little goals each week and if I improve on those things, then I know come Sunday I might have a chance."

Patrick's father gave him a set of plastic golf clubs when he was an infant. He took golf lessons when he was 9 years old. He played for Augusta State University. Later, he went on the PGA Tour.

"I remember my first couple of PGA Tour events. I didn't play particularly well. My first two events -- the FedEx St. Jude Classic and Frys.com Open -- I got killed."

So, what did he do? "I was trying to play a different kind of golf than I normally do, trying to kill it and hit all these shots."

"I learned quickly that you have to play the way you play. That's how I have been playing ever since."

"I've just learned to not worry about anything else and see where I want to get to and go get it," says Patrick.

Getting in the zone is important to Patrick. "At tournaments, you'll see me put in my headphones and get in my zone."

Patrick sees himself as a determined man. "I'm passionate and determined about golf."

And, Patrick has said, "I'm also a fun-loving guy who loves his family and hanging out."

So, what does he think about having confidence?

"I'm confident and have a belief in myself, and if you don't have that belief, you're never going to succeed."

Some people sometimes call Patrick "overconfident and cocky." He says he handles that by just knowing, "That's their opinion."

Patrick points out, "Some say there's a borderline between being confident and being cocky but at the end of the day you have to believe in yourself and be confident."

"Winning is fun... Sure. "But winning is not the point. Wanting to win is the point. Not giving up is the point. Never letting up is the point. Never being satisfied with what you've done is the point."

-Pat Summitt

22. THE CONFIDENCE ELEVATOR.

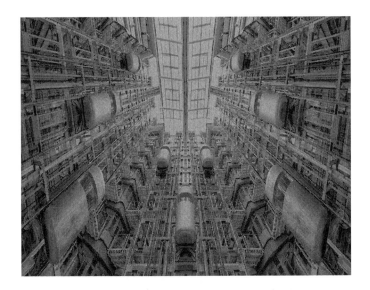

Jack Nicklaus wasn't a great golfer overnight. He worked at it.

If you won an event or a tournament, you may feel temporarily confident. Then again, losing the next tournament may lower your confidence.

Having confidence only when you win is like being in an elevator that goes up when you win, and down when you lose.

Winners need confidence that remains inside themselves - win or lose.

Like Justin Thomas explained, "It's knowing you can get past the bad shots, that you're better than that.

Many prominent psychologists have written articles in Psychology Today and prescribe various ways on "How to increase confidence, whether you win or lose."

These are some of the recommended ways:

> "See yourself as a top-level golfer training and working hard to be the next great player. Visualize yourself reaching that goal. Let your brain guide you to that goal."

> "Accept that you, like everyone else, make mistakes."

> "Realize you are growing every day. You gain confidence from training and learning from mistakes."

> ➢ Keep saying to yourself the optimistic autosuggestion words of the French Psychologist, Emile Coue,

> *"Every day, in every way, I am getting better and better."*

> ➢ "Determine (and ask friends too) what your best character traits are. Be quietly proud of them. Draw confidence from the good things about yourself every day."

It's easy to be skeptical, but tell yourself you are going to be positive and train, and your brain will automatically lead you there.

Know it isn't easy.

Think this way for at least one month. Then reflect back and you'll see a difference.

23. "I NEVER UNDERESTIMATE MY OPPONENT, BUT I NEVER UNDERESTIMATE MY OWN TALENTS." - Hale Irwin

"He's the best ball striker I ever saw."

"I once saw him hit a one-yard draw. On purpose!"
- Nick Faldo, talking about Hale Irwin.

Hal's modest reply: "That's nice of Nick, but that was back when you could really move the Balata ball"

During the 1970s and 1980s, Hale Irwin was a force to be reckoned with on Tour. He'd won three majors and had 84 other professional wins.

When Mark O'Meara began playing the tour. He played an event with Hal, but, Mark played badly. After the round, Mark, not knowing any better, apologized to Hale for his bad play.

Hal was taken aback and replied, "I don't give a damn how you played. I was only and totally concerned how I played."

Hal tells young golfers considering a career on tour, "I've felt that if you dwell too much on your errors, you're dealing in the negativity of things. I don't like that."

Hal recommends to young golfers, "I'd rather work on the positive reinforcement, the things you do well."

Before tournaments, Hal says, "If you're not just a little bit nervous before a match, you probably don't have the expectations of yourself that you should have."

And, "People have to learn who they are - you can't have somebody else telling you who you are."

Hal attended the University of Colorado where he was an academic All American, and a two time All-Big Eight Defensive back on the University of Colorado football team.

He talks about having courage, "Do I want to tackle a 230-pound guy who's running like a deer?"

Hal said, "Heavens no, no one in their right mind would."

But, Hal had something inside himself that drove him. "There is something that drives me and compels me to stick my head in there and give it my best shot and tackle the 230-pound guy."

And if you can't keep cool on the course, Hal has said, "Let your emotions come out. If your behavior is flat, your game will be flat, too."

Hal's best quick tip for golfers who for some unknown reason began to play bad during a round is,

"The best quick tip in golf is to focus on your rhythm and balance."

Finally, Hal says at no time should you ever get down on yourself no matter what you decide to do with your life.

"People, in whatever walk of life, would be surprised if they just gave themselves a chance by believing in what they are."

24. "NEVER LET UP." - Sam Snead.

"Sam Snead will fly anywhere in my plane with me."

"Sam's not as worried about the danger as he is about saving money."

> *-Arnold Palmer*

"Slammin' Sammy" Snead never let up.

He explained, "The more you can win by, the more doubts you put in the other players' minds the next time out."

Sam still holds the record for winning more PGA Tour events than any other player with 82 wins on Tour, not mentioning his worldwide tournament wins totaling 165 during his career.

Sam said, "I began caddying at the age of 7 in Hot Springs, Virginia and later became the assistant pro there."

"I won the first professional tournament I ever played in, so I thought I'd play golf."

Sam, a country boy, said, "Golf got complicated when I had to wear shoes and begin thinking about what I was doing."

Sam had a golf swing as smooth as silk and had great common sense. "In golf, as in life, you get out of it what you put into it," said Sam.

He was conservative in his game. "Most people who play golf have one big trouble: they think too much."

Sam recommended, "To get any real mileage out of this game you've got to sit on your imagination."

"The mark of a great player is in his ability to come back. The great champions have all come back from defeat."

His advice on working on your game? "Correct one fault at a time. Concentrate on the one fault you want to overcome."

Sam recommends having a pre-shot routine and be decisive and confident about your choice.

"Make the basic shot-making decision early, clearly and firmly, and then ritualize all the necessary acts of preparation."

Sam said be confident. "You've got be fearless too, even if you're playing a course for the first time with hundreds of sand traps and water hazards everywhere."

He added, "Of all the hazards, fear is the worst."

Sam said to just play your own game. "Forget your opponents; always play against par."

And, Sam said to manage your play. "Don't just play your way around the course. *Think your way* around way around the course."

If you want consistency, Sam said, "You put distance between yourself and what happens to you on the golf course. This isn't indifference, it's detachment."

Sam practiced hard, "Practice puts brains in your muscles."

But don't take yourself too seriously. Sam said, "The only reason I ever played golf in the first place was so I could afford to hunt and fish."

And, never give up. "No matter what happens - never give up a hole."

"It's like tossing in your cards after a bad beginning."

Sam humorously added, "You undermine your whole game, because to quit between tee and green is more habit-forming than drinking a highball before breakfast."

Sam's best advice for young golfers is not to think down on themselves. "You have more potential than you think, and keep close count of your nickels and dimes, stay away from whiskey, and never concede a putt."

25. "EVERY DAY THAT YOU DON'T PRACTICE IS ONE DAY LONGER BEFORE YOU ACHIEVE GREATNESS." – Ben Hogan.

""Ben was a little bitty fellow, so they'd throw him to the back of the line, that's how he got so mean."

-Gardner Dickenson

Ben Hogan grew up in a poor family. His father died when he was nine.

Ben delivered newspapers, Then, worked as a caddy in Texas. He practiced a lot and eventually won all four major championships.

"Practicing is very important," said Ben.

He spent hours on the driving range and usually practiced alone. He practiced much longer than most. "There are no shortcuts on the quest for perfection," he said.

Ben also is credited with the famous quote about practicing, "The more I practice, the luckier I get."

And don't be concerned if you hit bad shots." Ben explained, "Golf is not a game of good shots. It's a game of bad shots."

And he really meant, what many say, "The best players in golf learn how to hit the best bad shots."

Hogan wasn't concerned about socializing on the golf course. When he competed, he gave complete concentration to the game.

For example, on the first tee, Hogan said to the player he'd been paired with the day before and told him, "I'm sorry I didn't speak to you yesterday."

Then he continued by saying, "But just so you're not surprised, I won't be saying anything today either."

Sam Snead said, "About all Ben ever said in a tournament was "Good luck" on the 1st tee, and 'You're away' after that."

He didn't say much, but he did give guidance on what you should do if you can't beat a competitor that day. "If you can't outplay them, outwork them."

"To be a champ you have to believe in yourself when no one else will."

- Sugar Ray Robinson

26. "CONFIDENCE IN GOLF MEANS BEING ABLE TO CONCENTRATE ON THE PROBLEM AT HAND WITH NO OUTSIDE INTEREFERENCE." - Tom Watson

"Tom Watson, he'll hit the ball in the trees and undaunted go in there, flail it out and make something out of it."

> *- Gary McCord*

Tom Watson won eight major championships. He led the Tour money list five times. He was ranked number one in the world for several years.

He began playing competitive golf in high school in Kansas City.

He had a turning point in his life at that time.

"I have a special feeling for Blue Hills CC, where I won perhaps the most important tournament of my life when I was 14 - the Kansas City Match Play Championship."

"That win gave me a dream of becoming a professional golfer."

He then won four Missouri State Amateur championships, 1967, 1968, 1970 and 1971.

Tom was competitive for years. "I led the 2nd and 3rd rounds of The Open at the age of 59, but lost in a playoff."

But age takes its toll. "Golfers who play a lot of courses often encounter short ledges or retaining walls they climb over."

"When I was younger, I always had fun hopping down from them."

"I could jump off a wall six feet high and land like a cat, no problem."

"Well, today I can't jump off anything higher than two feet without it just killing me."

Tom keeps a positive realistic attitude. "I guess I have never been much of a complainer."

Tom explained, "You just take what is given you, and don't complain about what you can't affect."

He's satisfied with that. "I'm very happy with my life. I am what I am. I don't worry about anything that I can't control. That's a really good lesson in life."

Tom can handle pressure with a realistic attitude. "Some guys have trouble sleeping the night before an important round. I never have."

"Invariably, I sleep longer and better, and have more dreams, when I'm in contention and feeling pressure."

As a realist, he knows he doesn't like to lose. "I've said many times, 'You learn to win through not liking to lose.' And that's what I mean by learning how to win."

When you have walked the walk, you know talk is just talk. "A lot of guys who have never choked have never been in the position to do so."

As Tom looked back on his career, he said, "My career was one of just taking it step by step."

Tom added, "I didn't know how I was gonna fare on the professional circuit when I qualified. I didn't know whether I was gonna make a dime."

Tom explained, "I didn't know anything but this one thing: I had some dreams, and I was gonna work harder than anybody out here to ply my trade."

Tom loves the game.

"The beautiful thing about the game of golf is you can play good golf and compete well into your later years, and you can't do this in basketball or football or baseball."

Finally, to young golfers, his advice is clear. "Golf is a game of ego, but it is also a game of integrity: the most important thing is, *you do what is right when no one is looking.*"

"I follow three rules: Do the right thing, do the best you can, and always show people you care."

- Lou Holtz

27. "I LOOK INTO THEIR EYES, SHAKE THEIR HANDS, PAT THEIR BACK AND WISH THEM LUCK, BUT I AM THINKING, I AM GOING TO BURY YOU." – Seve Ballesteros

"Seve wore his emotions on his sleeve. You could see how much the guy cared about winning."

- Johnny Miller

Seve also said, "If you ever feel sorry for somebody on a golf course, you'd better go home. If you don't kill them, they'll kill you."

His uncle was a four-time Spanish National Champion who also finished 6th in The Masters. His older brothers were professional golfers.

Seve said about his childhood, "I was the youngest of five sons and grew up in Spain and learned golf playing on the beaches near my home."

His older brothers were professional golfers.

"I turned pro when I was 16 and played in The Open at Royal Birkdale and finished second the first time I ever played."

He later won The Masters twice and The Open three times.

He didn't give up. He was intense. "The only time I talk on the golf course is to my caddie."

Seve added, "And then only to complain when he gives me the wrong club."

He was very well liked, but very competitive.

"To give yourself the best possible chance of playing to your potential, you must prepare for every eventuality. That means practice."

He had a great attitude. "I know where I am and I know which way I'm going, ... Only winning will satisfy me. You don't think it is possible? It is very possible."

He was criticized since he found the bunkers often. He didn't let the critics bother him about that. "They say I get into too many bunkers. But is no problem. I am the best bunker player."

When the fairways were narrow, he kept that positive attitude. "I'd like to see the fairways narrower."

Narrower?

Seve explained, "Then everyone would have to play from the rough, not just me."

Seve was diagnosed with a brain tumor and underwent several operations to remove the tumor but passed away a few years later in his 50s.

He always kept a positive and realistic attitude. "For everything in life there is always a beginning and an end."

He knew he wasn't getting better and said, "This is the tough part, the most difficult thing, when you see that it's coming: The end."

It is what it is.

Seve was hard to impress. "I see a lot of great players with great talent and a great future ahead. But impress me? I'm not that easily impressed."

And he didn't make a big deal out of things. Being interviewed on how he four-putted at the Masters, he gave his own "slightly sarcastic" and "complicated and detailed" analysis of his four-putt, "I miss the putt. I miss the putt. I miss the putt. I make."

"Self-praise is for losers. Be a winner."

"Stand for something."

"Always have class, and be humble."

- John Madden

28. "THINK ABOUT THE DISTANCE YOU WANT THE BALL TO FLY, AND ONLY THAT NUMBER." - Rickie Fowler

"He just keeps fighting. That's what I love about this kid. There's no quitting in him."

> *- Butch Harmon*

"My first years on tour, I tried to be super professional by considering the yardages to every feature and hazard."

"Over time, my caddie and I noticed I play better when we keep it simple."

Rickie and his caddie decided the way to keep it really simple is to, "Think about the distance you want the ball to fly, and only that number."

Rickie began playing golf when his grandfather took him to the driving range when he was two years old.

"My grandpa was the one; he started taking up golf when I was about two and introduced me to the game as far as just taking me to the driving range where I grew up playing."

Rickie discovered he had a talent for visualizing a golf shot.

"My grandpa would take me to the driving range and, I don't know, it didn't take me long to realize I'm a little different with golf. I have an eye for seeing things differently. Somehow, I just see shots in my head."

"That was really all he had to do was let me hit a golf ball and I kind of fell in love with it from there."

"He didn't really have to teach me a whole lot," said Rickie.

Rickie's parents encouraged him. "I come from great stock."

"I didn't come from money," said Rickie.

"My parents both worked really hard to keep food on the table and give my sister and I opportunities to play sports to see what we were good at."

"Mom always got me to school, and the driving range while Dad was working. She also kept me quiet and humble."

"Both of them taught me to let my golf do the talking," said Rickie.

"One of the main rules with my mom was if I broke a club, she was going to take it and I wouldn't get it back. So, I made sure I kept all my clubs."

Rickie loved to compete in Motocross.

"On a dirt bike, when you're sizing up a jump, you can't have any second thoughts. You have to fully commit. If you don't, a lot of things can go wrong."

The same applies to deciding on a golf shot.

"The way I see it, thinking about the position of the club during the swing is about the worst way to play golf."

Too much thought isn't good. "It makes you tight and defensive, which kills your natural speed and rhythm," Rickie said.

Rickie added, "I'm one of a few guys on the PGA Tour who doesn't work with an instructor."

"I'm not saying mechanics don't matter," Rickie explained.

"But I play my best when I focus on staying in a good place mentally and keep the technique simple."

Keeping things simple works for Rickie but slow play can be a problem but his advice for dealing with slow play is also simple.

"It's harder to score well in a slow round."

"The tendency is to overthink shots while you're waiting and become mentally exhausted."

"Instead, chat with your playing partners about anything but golf. Concentrate on each shot for no more than a minute. You'll stay fresh."

Rickie talked about his transition to the PGA Tour.

"Time management is probably the biggest thing I've had to learn to deal with being on the PGA Tour, whether it be media or figuring out how many weeks to play in a row. That's been the biggest adjustment, coming from amateur golf."

Rickie knows the young fans are drawn to him.

"It's great to be somewhat of a role model," Rickie said.

"I want to be a positive and good role model and lead by example and try to do the best I can."

Rickie added, "Playing good golf definitely draws attention, but I want to have a good attitude on the course and do the right things."

29. "MY FATHER TAUGHT ME THE GAME AND HE ALWAYS STRESSED THE FUN OF PLAYING," said Peter Jacobsen

"Peter Jacobsen was the guy that, at the roundtable or the lunchroom or something, he would sit down, introduce himself to four or five young guys that he didn't even know and say, 'If I was you and I was starting my pro career, this is a list of things I would think about,'"

- Brian Henninger

Peter was asked, "What do younger pros say to distinguished veterans like you?"

Peter replied, "I was walking all the way back to the tournament tee during a Wednesday Pro Am at one hole and I hear, 'Hey, old man, where are you going? Your senior tees are up here.' Yeah, yeah, keep smiling there, funny boy.'"

Peter Jacobsen, with 22 professional wins, is one of the finest commentators on the Golf Channel and NBC Sports.

He's won two majors on the Champions Tour.

He played college golf and said, "I turned professional in 1976 after winning the Oregon Open."

Peter responded to our request when we asked him what inspired him to decide on a golf career.

Peter said, "My father taught me the game and he always stressed the fun of playing and being with my friends and family on the course."

"It was always about spending that special time with family and friends. Golf taught me self-reliance, taking responsibility and honesty."

One of his most famous statements about the nature of golf is, "One of the most fascinating things about golf is how it reflects the cycle of life."

"No matter what you shoot - the next day you have to go back to the first tee and begin all over again and make yourself into something."

He has a witty and laid back personality and enjoys life. "If you can't enjoy the time between golf shots, then you are going to have a pretty difficult life because most of your life is the time spent in-between."

His personality stood out early on tour as he was adept at doing impressions of his competitors. He imitated them perfectly.

Peter believes you don't have to have a perfect golf swing.

"The Golf Hall of Fame is full of players with unusual looking swings."

Unusual is okay, of course. Pretty may or may not be effective. "Some of the prettiest swings you've ever seen in your life are made on the far end of the public driving range by guys who couldn't break an egg with a baseball bat," Peter said.

Peter's advised young golfers to have confidence.

"Your confidence is the 15th club in your bag. You'd like it to be a thick-headed driver. But it sometimes seems like a pretty weak little stick."

So, work at your confidence and read the last Chapter of this book several times.

Peter maintained his confidence over his long career.

He beat the best players in the world at the age of 49 when he won the Greater Hartford Open in 2003 and was voted the Tour's Comeback Player of the Year.

"Strong people don't put others down… they lift them up."

– Michael P. Watson, Commonwealth Middleweight Boxing Champion 1989-91

30. "WHEN I'M PLAYING MY BEST AND FIND MYSELF IN CONTENTION ON SUNDAYS, IT'S USUALLY WHEN I'M NOT THINKING ABOUT MY SWING, BUT RATHER TRUSTING MY SETUP UP AND SLOWLY PULLING THE TRIGGER," said Sergio Garcia

"Sergio is a terrific golfer. A very fine gentleman."

"I love the way he's played all over the world."

"If you want to be recognized as the best golfer in the world, you've got to play worldwide."

- Gary Player

Victor Garcia, a Spanish golf pro, taught his son, Sergio, how to play golf beginning when Sergio was three years old.

He did very well as an amateur and turned professional at 19.

"Leading a tournament, especially a major, on Sunday is pressure," said Sergio.

"The best players in the world are after you wanting to win as much as you do."

Sergio didn't let the pressure get to him as he played the final round at the 2017 Masters in the last group.

During his interview after winning the tournament he said, "I haven't felt this calm before playing the course."

He explained, years ago, he loved playing the Augusta course the first time he played it, but then as the years went by, he wasn't thrilled about playing there.

When he finally won in 2017, he said, "I was supported by my friends and family during the tournament and just felt calm during the whole round."

"Justin is a good friend of mine and we both wanted to beat the other rather than have the other lose it."

He won after the final round, and walked the round in a calm and confident manner which allowed his subconscious to let all his talent surface.

Sergio proved his attitude toward "Trusting his set up and slowly pulling the trigger," works very well under a pressure situation.

Sergio added, "I won't completely rely on feel - I like to keep a few images of the shots I'm going to make in the back of my mind to make sure that I get the most out of my driver, irons and wedges."

Sergio said, "I've always felt I should do things 100 percent or not do them. It's all or nothing."

Sergio explained, "That's what makes me a good athlete - doing things with all the 'ganas' I can."

Sergio said, you need to keep positive.

"Obviously, the good thing about golf, it's difficult to really, really blow it after five holes, unless it goes really, really, really... really, really, really wrong."

"You still have 13 to go, and if you have a good run, where you make five or six birdies, you can get it back somehow."

Sergio has advised young golfers in the past to make sure you take the right stance with the right club.

"Your woods, irons and wedges are built with specific lengths and lie angles, which demand that you stand to the ball a little differently for each one."

He adds, "The secret is to know which elements of your address position remain constant, and which ones you have to tweak to match the club in your hand."

He finds it best not to be too serious in a round.

"To concentrate intensely for 4 and a half hours, that's too hard for me. Too tiring."

So, instead he says to, "I concentrate 'lo maximo' on the 'golpe,' (i.e. the stroke), but between strokes I'm interacting with the crowd or laughing with my caddie, and talking about the spectators."

His positive and relaxed attitude paid off when he drove it under an azalea bush on the par 5 13th hole, and wound up parring the hole, while Justin

Rose missed a makeable putt for birdie and settled for par.

Having friends is important to Sergio.

"I can count my close friends on two hands, which is good, I think. That's a lot."

"Some of my friends are at home in Spain, others are elsewhere, and some are in golf."

Sergio's advice to young golfers who want to hit the big drive is:

"When it comes to hitting solid drives, the secret is to swing within yourself."

"I know that sounds like a cliché, but it's true."

"If you swing at 100 miles per hour and hit it on the toe, you won't hit the ball as far as you would with an 80-mph swing that catches the ball in the center of the clubface."

Sergio added, "Copy my favorite moves and my Tour-proven setup positions, and you'll start catching it on the sweet spot every time, with every club in your bag.

Finally, Sergio said it's important to have a positive competitive attitude. "I am competitive, and I like to be as competitive as possible in anything I do."

31. "I PLAYED SMART AND I MISSED SMART, JUST KEEP PLAYING LIKE THAT," said Jon Rahm

"Every part of his game is a strength. I think he's one of the best players in the world."

> *- Phil Mickleson*

Jon Rahm-Rodriguez was born in a small town in Spain and played golf for Arizona State University.

"My father wanted me to play golf in America," said Jon.

"I wanted to play golf since I was a child because of the example set by Seve Ballesteros and Jose Maria Olazabal."

Coached by Tim Mickleson (Phil's brother), Jon said, "I've played a lot with Phil."

"He told me even before I turned pro that he thought I was one of the top 10 best players in the world."

Jon added, "I was like, 'okay, he's just trying to be nice, right? It's not possible.'"

"But, you know, once I turned pro, I started believing he was right. I'm pretty close to getting to that point."

Jon had 11 collegiate tournaments, second only to Phil Mickleson who had 16.

"I turned pro in 2016, after being low amateur at the US Open."

His success came early. "I won the Farmers Insurance Open this year (2017) making a long eagle putt on the final hole."

Later, he was in a semifinal match against Dustin Johnson, the number one player in the world in the World Golf Championship in Mexico and things started to go wrong.

Young golfers can learn from Jon's positive attitude in learning from his loss:

"I couldn't control my body, honestly."

"I don't know, it was like my body was independent from my mind."

"I was trying to focus and do my routine, but things just weren't happening," Jon said.

"If I had been a little luckier on 17 and 18, maybe I would have had a chance to score in the match or go into a playoff."

"But the damage was already done." Jon said.

"I tried my hardest."

"But I learned that, you know, if I'm having a good day, I can face the No. 1 player in the world."

Even though he lost, Jon learned from trying hard he could face the best and gained confidence from experiencing he could play fairly well against D.J.

Some are calling Jon the "Next Nicklaus" and he's off to a great start with that positive attitude and learning from his loss to D.J.

Before he started the Masters, Jon said, "If I didn't think I could win it, I wouldn't be here."

Jon's belief in his own ability continues. He said, "I do feel like I belong here, that I belong where I am right now."

32. "WALK THE WINNING WAYS"

There are lots of ways to raise your confidence level. Many psychologists believe the following are various ways to raise your self-esteem and confidence and maintain a good confidence level:

> ➢ MAKE TWO LISTS:

"Determine as accurately as you can what your strengths are in golf, and what you've accomplished so far."

"Then make two separate lists: 1) the first list is what you believe your strengths are (and ask another person who knows you for help in making your list of your golf strengths)."

2). "On the second list, write down your accomplishments whether they be events, tournaments, or rounds of golf or shots on the range."

"Include in the second list all small (no matter how small), medium and large successes you've accomplished so far."

"Review the first list as a list of abilities you have and update it from time to time as you practice and get better."

"View the second list of accomplishments as confidence building events. Don't disregard listing any of your achievements no matter how small."

"Review each list every week and keep updating it. Each event you list helps you to attain more confidence."

➤ WRITE DOWN YOUR GOALS AND TRAINING SCHEDULE.

"Make a realistic description of your goals you want to reach and the training you will do to reach each goal."

➤ VISUALIZE. "Visualize yourself reaching these goals and try to be as realistic as you can. Being realistic is better than being overconfident."

➤ TRAIN: "Keep in mind how training and hard work will transform you. Consistent training is better than inconsistent training."

➤ AVOID NEGATIVE PEOPLE: "Avoid people or situations which give you negative input."

"Negative people (even if you discount what they say) will not help your confidence. Seek the positive people and positive events."

"Deal with critical people as giving you an opportunity to grow. Don't take good faith criticism negatively. It's really good faith advice on how to grow."

"Disregard bad faith or jealous criticism."

➢ LEARN FROM MISTAKES: "Realize every disappointment you may encounter on the golf course is an opportunity to learn."

➢ YOU'RE NOT A LOSER: "Don't ever tell yourself you're a loser or you can't do it. You are a unique wonderful person."

➢ DRESS UP: "Care for yourself better. Wear nice clothes, keep yourself well-groomed."

➢ DON'T SLOUCH: "Keep your head raised looking straight ahead when you walk the course."

➢ EXERCISE: "Exercise reduces stress and exercise at least three times a week."

➢ BE KIND: "Do kind things for the people around you and smile more. This will make you feel better about yourself."

- ➢ BELIEVE IN YOURSELF: "If you don't believe you can win, your mind will keep you from winning. Have faith in yourself and keep positive."

- ➢ PRE-SHOT ROUTINE: "A pre-shot routine will make you focus on what is happening now so you won't be thinking about the future or the past as you cannot think of more than one thing at a time. Have no worries about the future, i.e. how the shot will turn out."

- ➢ RELAX: "Compose yourself and act confidently and you will be confident. Be aware that negative thoughts will tense up your muscles."

- ➢ YOU DID IT BEFORE AND YOU'LL DO IT AGAIN: "Let your confident mind take over your body. You've made good shots before and you'll make good shots again."

- ➢ DON'T CRITICIZE YOURSELF: "If you find your mind criticizing yourself, tell yourself you definitely have the ability not to make those mistakes."

➢ KNOW YOU ARE GROWING: "Remind yourself with each shot you are continually gaining knowledge and experience in golf and are becoming a better golfer."

➢ FORGET ABOUT COMPETITORS: "Don't concern or worry yourself with thoughts of what other competitors are doing. Know they may be worrying about you."

➢ VISUALIZE EACH SHOT: "Visualize the shot and have a clear picture in your mind of the shot you are going to make."

➢ TAKE A MOMENT TO BE SURE OF A SHOT. "If you feel unsure about the shot, take a step back and visualize another shot you feel more confident about."

➢ HOW TO HANDLE BAD SHOTS: "When bad shots happen (be aware they will happen), don't dwell on it. Good and bad shots are bound to happen. Stay positive and comfortable."

➢ TAKE DEEP BREATHS TO CALM YOURSELF: "If you feel yourself flustered, stop and take deep breaths to get more oxygen to your brain."

➢ DON'T GIVE UP: "Some players start to give up on themselves after a series of bad shots."

"Instead of giving up, ask yourself what the cause might be – usually it's some small error or event which you might be overly exaggerating in your mind."

➢ ENCOURAGE YOURSELF: "Tell yourself, errors happen but you still have your ability and the hours of practicing and experience behind you. So, smile and feel great about yourself no matter what."

➢ STAY CALM. "Don't look at your golf round as trying to achieve a low score. You can't automatically do anything to undo bad holes.

Remember what the famous Psychologist, Philosopher and Physician, William James said, "We become what we think of most of the time."

Keep a positive view of yourself. You will become what you want to be. Enjoy!

"When you have confidence, you can have a lot of fun."

"And when you have fun, you can do amazing things."

-Joe Namath

"Don't wait until everything is just right."

"It will never be perfect."

"There will always be challenges, obstacles and less than perfect conditions."

"So, what…."

"Get started now."

"With each step you take, you will grow stronger and stronger, more and more skilled, more and more self-confident and more and more successful."

-Mark Victor Hansen

Thank you for taking an interest in our book. We hope you enjoyed it and please consider leaving a review on Amazon so more readers can find this title.

A final message to you from The Team at Golfwell:

Above all, have fun playing golf and enjoy all your adventures! Thank you for reading and best to you!

More about the Team at Golfwell >

https://www.amazon.com/The-Team-at-Golfwell/e/B01CFW4EQG

Made in the USA
San Bernardino, CA
19 December 2018